The symbols in the book tell you whether the animal is:

Vertebrate ■ or invertebrate □
Warm blooded ▲ or cold blooded △
Nocturnal ▬ or diurnal ▭
and whether the animal has babies (young born alive) ● or lays eggs ○ .

If there is no symbol ▬ or ▭ it means that the animal sometimes sleeps in the day and sometimes at night.

Scientists classify animals into groups.
The animals in this encyclopaedia fit into the following groups:

mollusc   crustacean   arachnid

insect   fish   amphibian

reptile   bird   mammal

Some of the words you may not understand are explained in the glossary on page 70 in Volume 4.

Adder

Scientific name
Vipera berus

reptile

■ Vertebrate △ Cold blooded ● Young born alive ▢ Diurnal

The adder is a poisonous snake. It kills its prey with one bite of its poisonous fangs. It has a dark zig zag pattern on its back. This warns other animals to keep away.

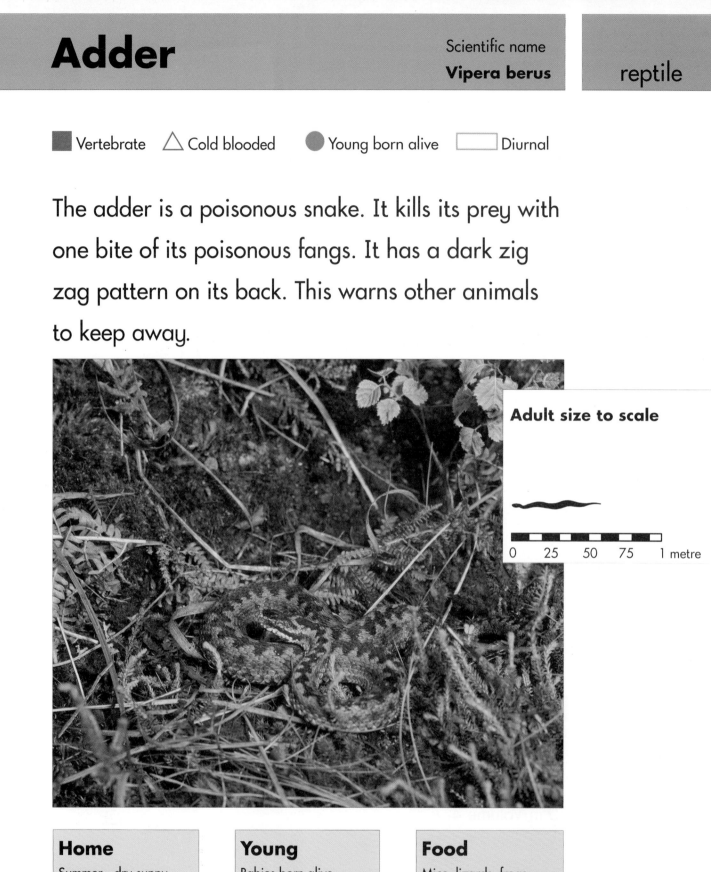

Adult size to scale

0   25   50   75   1 metre

Home
Summer - dry sunny open spaces.
Winter - hibernates underground.

Young
Babies born alive, up to 15 at a time.

Food
Mice, lizards, frogs.

Ant

Black garden Ant

Scientific name

Lasius niger

insect

☐ Invertebrate   △ Cold blooded   ◯ Lays eggs   ▭ Diurnal

Ants live in a large group called a colony. In the colony each ant has a special job to do. The queen's job is to lay the eggs. The workers' job is to find food and bring it back to the colony.

Actual adult size
The queen is much larger.

Home
Meadows, gardens.
Nests under the ground.

Young
Queen lays hundreds of eggs.

Food
Sweet things.

Badger

Scientific name
Meles meles

mammal

■ Vertebrate ▲ Warm blooded ● Young born alive ▨ Nocturnal

The badger has strong legs and claws which make it good at digging. It builds an underground home with rooms and tunnels and several ways in and out. At night the badger comes out to feed and play.

Adult size to scale

0   25   50   75   1 metre

Home
Woodland.
Underground sett.

Young
2 or 3 babies (cubs)
in a litter.

Food
Worms, insects, honey
from bees' nests.

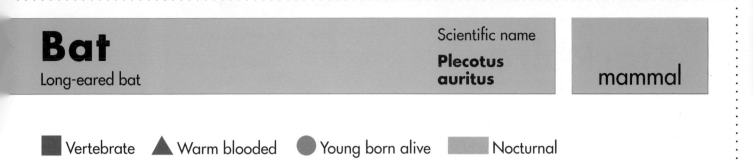

Bat
Long-eared bat

Scientific name
Plecotus auritus

mammal

■ Vertebrate ▲ Warm blooded ● Young born alive ▮ Nocturnal

The bat hunts at night. It finds its prey by sending out a shrill squeak. This bounces off the prey and back to the bat's ears. In the daytime it hangs upside down, holding on with its toes.

Adult size to scale

0   25   50   75   1 metre

Home
Open spaces, roof spaces.
Hibernates in winter.

Young
One baby born a year.
Young can fly when one week old.

Food
Insects, grubs.

Blackbird

Scientific name
Turdus merula

bird

■ Vertebrate ▲ Warm blooded ○ Lays eggs ▢ Diurnal

Only the male blackbird has black feathers. The female has brown feathers. Blackbirds are good songbirds. If an enemy is near, blackbirds make a loud noise. This noise can warn other birds and frighten away the enemy.

Adult size to scale

0   25   50   75   1 metre

Home
Woodland, parks, gardens.
Nests in bushes.

Young
3 to 5 blue-green speckled eggs.

Food
Worms, berries, fallen apples.

6

Bluebottle

Scientific name
Calliphora vomitoria

insect

☐ Invertebrate   △ Cold blooded   ◯ Lays eggs   ☐ Diurnal

Bluebottles are big blue buzzing flies. They eat dead and rotting things and they also eat our food. They spread germs by walking on our food and vomiting on it. Female bluebottles sometimes lay their eggs on our food.

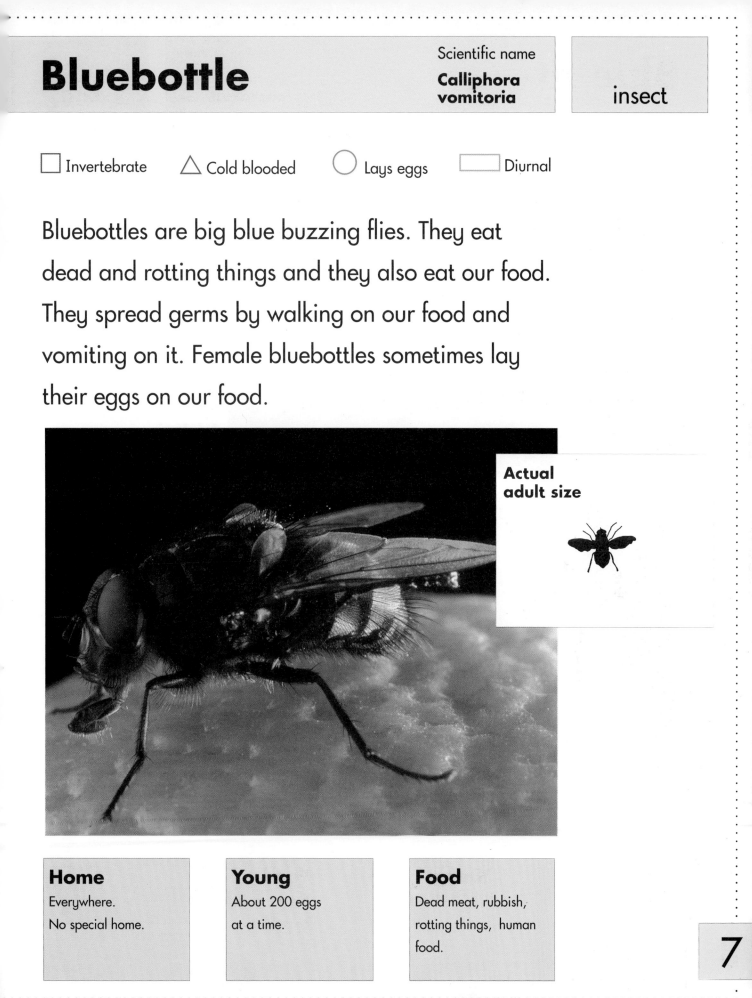

Actual adult size

Home
Everywhere.
No special home.

Young
About 200 eggs
at a time.

Food
Dead meat, rubbish,
rotting things, human
food.

7

Blue tit

Scientific name

Parus caeruleus

bird

■ Vertebrate   ▲ Warm blooded   ◯ Lays eggs   ▭ Diurnal

The blue tit is often seen in gardens. It is a good little acrobat and it can hang upside down by its toes. It has learnt how to peck through milk bottle tops so that it can drink the cream.

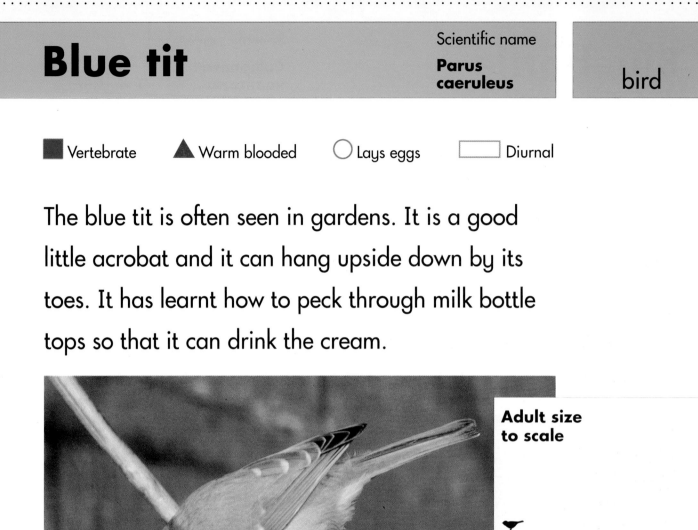

Adult size to scale

| 0 | 25 | 50 | 75 | 1 metre |

Home
Woodland, gardens. Nests in hollow trees, nest boxes.

Young
7 to 12 white speckled eggs.

Food
Insects, grubs, nuts, coconut, bacon rind.

Bumble Bee
Buff-tailed bumble bee

Scientific name
Bombus terrestris

insect

☐ Invertebrate   △ Cold blooded   ◯ Lays eggs   ▭ Diurnal

The bumble bee is a large, striped bee. If it feels it is in danger it can sting. The loud buzzing noise and the yellow and black colours of the bumble bee are a warning to animals to keep away.

Actual adult size
The queen is larger

Home
Open spaces.
Nests under the ground.

Young
Queen lays about 150 eggs.

Food
Nectar and pollen from flowers.

☐ Invertebrate   △ Cold blooded   ○ Lays eggs   ☐ Diurnal

The peacock butterfly has a special pattern on its wings. This pattern looks like a pair of eyes. This frightens away predators who think they are seeing the eyes of a big animal.

Adult size to scale

0   25   50   75   1 metre

Home
Open land, gardens. Hibernates in dark places like sheds.

Young
200 eggs laid on nettle leaves. Hatch into caterpillars.

Food
Caterpillars eat nettle leaves.
Butterflies eat nectar.

Cod

Scientific name

Gadus morhua

fish

■ Vertebrate △ Cold blooded ○ Lays eggs

Fishermen catch millions of cod every year. Cod usually live in the deepest, coldest water at the bottom of the sea. Cod are scavengers. With their strong teeth they can eat almost anything.

Adult size to scale

| 0 | 25 | 50 | 75 | 1 metre |

Home
Sea water 600m deep.

Young
Lays 2 to 3 million eggs.

Food
Crabs, prawns, other fish. Anything it can find.

Scientific name
Carcinus maenas

crustacean

☐ Invertebrate   △ Cold blooded   ○ Lays eggs

The crab has sharp pincers and four pairs of legs. It also has a hard shell to protect itself. When it is frightened a crab runs away. It always runs sideways.

Adult size to scale

0   25   50   75   1 metre

Home	**Young**	**Food**
Seashore, under rocks.	Female lays 3000 to 4000 eggs. Carries them until they hatch.	Dead sea creatures.

Cranefly

Scientific name

Tipula paludosa

insect

☐ Invertebrate △ Cold blooded ○ Lays eggs

The cranefly has six very long legs. So another name for the cranefly is Daddy long legs. It can shed its legs if it needs to get away from an enemy.

Actual adult size

Home
Grassy places, gardens.

Young
Lays 50 to 150 eggs.

Food
Grubs eat roots of plants.
Adults eat liquids only.

Cricket

Dark bush cricket

Scientific name
Pholidoptera griseoaptera

insect

☐ Invertebrate   △ Cold blooded   ○ Lays eggs

Crickets have strong back legs which make them good at hopping out of danger. They also have wings and can fly. The male rubs his wings together to make a buzzing noise. This noise tells other crickets where he is.

Actual adult size

Home
Grassy places, edges of woodland.

Young
Eggs laid one at a time in rotten wood.

Food
Plants, soft insects, grubs.

14

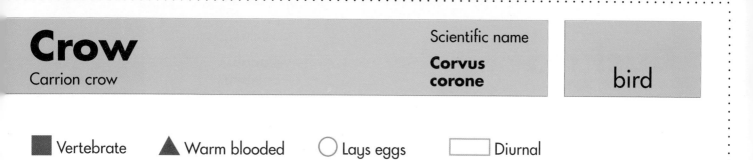

Crow
Carrion crow

Scientific name
Corvus corone

bird

■ Vertebrate ▲ Warm blooded ○ Lays eggs ▭ Diurnal

The carrion crow makes a `caw caw' sound. It eats dead animals, which are called carrion. It also eats other birds' eggs. The crow steals eggs and drops them onto the ground to smash them open.

Adult size to scale

0   25   50   75   1 metre

Home
Woodland, farmland.
Nests in tall trees.

Young
4 to 6 speckled eggs.

Food
Carrion, eggs, seeds, insects, worms.

Cuckoo

Scientific name
Cuculus canorus

bird

■ Vertebrate ▲ Warm blooded ○ Lays eggs ▭ Diurnal

The cuckoo is unusual because she lays her eggs in another bird's nest. Then she leaves the egg and flies away. When the cuckoo chick hatches it does not want to share its food. So it pushes the other eggs and young out of the nest.

Adult size to scale

0   25   50   75   1 metre

Home
Woodland.
In winter it migrates to Africa.

Young
Speckly brown eggs.
12 eggs laid in a year.
1 egg in each nest.

Food
Insects, grubs.